If found, kindly return to:

Name: _____

Phone: _____

Greatly appreciated

THE STRESS-LESS LIFE GUIDE
SUMMERTIME OR ANYTIME

KIDS AND PARENTS

The simplest and most effective steps to a happier,
healthier, and successful life!

CREATED BY
Dr. DIANNA M. and GABRIELLA K.
The Mother and Daughter Team

On top of our current monthly donations, a percentage of sales from ALL of our books will support children with mental and other health issues, some YouTube channels, and animal shelters which are helping abused and homeless animals.

Printed in the United States of America

First Printing, 2018

ISBN 978-1-7322971-4-2

Stress-Less Way Publishing

Connect with us:

Email: team@stresslessway.com

www.stresslessway.com

Disclaimer

Presented below, The Stress-Less Life Guide was created for educational and learning purposes only. Our ultimate goal is to provide a useful aid for anyone, including parents, professionals, schoolteachers and doctors. It is never too late to be on the way to your own Stress-Less life. Integrating our practices and methods into your lives on a daily basis will allow you and your loved ones to cope with stress more intelligently. You will learn how to guide yourself to a more fulfilling and stressless life. You will be in charge of your health, happiness, and future success. By following these Guides, you will be inspired to share your newfound skills with many others along your path.

OTHER GUIDES IN THIS SERIES:

- **THE STRESS-LESS LIFE GUIDE - TEENS.**
- **THE STRESS-LESS LIFE GUIDE - KIDS AND PARENTS.**
- **THE STRESS-LESS LIFE GUIDE - ADULTS.**
- **THE STRESS-LESS LIFE GUIDE - SUMMERTIME OR ANYTIME - TEENS.**

ENJOY OUR:

NEWEST AND ONGOING SERIES OF INCREDIBLY INSPIRING STRESS-LESS COLORING BOOKS FOR DIFFERENT AGES.
These books include inspiring Quotes and Drawings from ACTUAL children and adults, some of whom have very challenging health issues.

WELCOME BACK!!!

HELLO AGAIN! WE MISSED YOU!

THE MOTHER AND DAUGHTER TEAM IS HERE.
WE ARE THRILLED TO SEE YOU BACK!

THE VACATION TIME IS FINALLY HERE!!!

THE GUIDE THAT YOU ARE HOLDING IN YOUR HANDS WILL HELP YOU TO STAY ON TRACK TO A HAPPY LIFE WITH LESS STRESS.

REMEMBER THE SAYING: *"PRACTICE MAKES PERFECT!"*

WE HOPE YOU WILL KEEP ENJOYING YOUR DAILY EXERCISES FROM THIS WORKBOOK.

YOU WILL DEFINITELY BE BETTER PREPARED TO DEAL WITH ANY PROBLEMS OR CONCERNS MORE INTELLIGENTLY THIS UPCOMING SCHOOL YEAR!

HAVE A HAPPY, HEALTHY, AND FUN VACATION!

LOVE AND PEACE

THE GAME RULES

STEPS TO A HAPPY AND "STRESS-LESS" LIFE:

STEP 1. THE MOMENT YOU FEEL SAD - TRY TO THINK OR DO SOMETHING THAT **ALWAYS MAKES YOU HAPPY AND PUTS A SMILE ON YOUR FACE**. IT CAN BE ANYTHING:
- TALK TO YOUR PARENTS. HAVE A NICE FACE-TO-FACE CONVERSATION. SHARE WITH THEM WHAT MADE YOU UPSET. THEY WILL ALWAYS MAKE YOU FEEL BETTER AND HELP YOU WITH YOUR PROBLEMS.
- HAVE FUN WITH YOUR FAMILY AND/OR FRIENDS.
- READ YOUR FAVORITE BOOK.
- DRAW/PAINT SOMETHING.
- PLAY WITH YOUR ANIMALS IF YOU HAVE ANY.
- LISTEN TO YOUR FAVORITE MUSIC.
- PLAY YOUR FAVORITE INSTRUMENT.
- THINK ABOUT SOMETHING FUNNY.
- GO OUTSIDE IF THE WEATHER IS NICE.
- WATCH A FUNNY MOVIE OR VIDEO.

IT'S ALL ABOUT **POSITIVE** DISTRACTIONS!

P.S. STAY AWAY FROM SOCIAL MEDIA PLEASE!

STEP 2. WHEN YOU HAVE FREE TIME, WRITE DAILY IN THIS JOURNAL THINGS THAT MADE YOU HAPPY AND THINGS THAT MADE YOU FEEL SAD. YOU CAN DO IT TOGETHER WITH YOUR PARENTS. THEY WILL ALWAYS POINT YOU IN THE RIGHT DIRECTION.

IF NOTHING MADE YOU SAD - **FANTASTIC!!!** ENJOY YOUR DAY AND
WRITE DOWN ONLY THE THINGS THAT MADE YOU HAPPY TODAY. I AM SURE THAT YOUR PARENTS WILL BE SO EXCITED TO HEAR ABOUT THAT TOO.

STEP 3. COME BACK TO THESE PAGES LATER IN THE WEEK. YOU WILL SEE FOR YOURSELF THAT MOST OF YOUR PROBLEMS WERE EITHER GONE/SOLVED OR FORGOTTEN BY NOW. THEY WEREN'T THAT IMPORTANT TO BEGIN WITH. ISN'T THAT AMAZING?!
BACK THEN, YOU WERE UPSET OVER NOTHING!!!

THAT IS IT!!!
EASY AS 1,2,3.
BY BEING A MASTER OF YOUR MIND, THOUGHTS, AND BEHAVIOR, YOU, AND ONLY YOU, WERE ABLE TO TURN A SAD DAY TO A HAPPY DAY!

P.S. IN THE FUTURE, THESE JOURNALS WILL BECOME PRICELESS MEMORIES AND LIFE LESSONS FOR YOU AND YOUR OWN CHILDREN.
(ASK YOUR PARENTS TO SAVE THEM FOR YOU.)

HELLO FROM THE FURRY FAMILY!

Hey there! Guess who is spending VACATION with YOU?!

Meet the boys: Frankie, Louis, Vinny, Gatsby, Charlie, and Hippy!!!
Meet the girls: Lola, Emma, Stella and Kekkei!!!

"We would love to **join The Mother and Daughter Team** to help you and other children to stay happy and healthy! Also, we are more than thrilled to **help** other homeless and abused **animals** to have loving humans, warm homes, and yummy food. Our silly faces will pop out here and there throughout your whole summertime! We hope we can put a big smile on your face and bring even more happiness into your life!
Have a great and exciting vacation!"

P.S. All these pictures are provided by our loving family and friends. **Yes!!** The precious Furry Family really belong to all of us!

LOVE AND PEACE

The Mother, Daughter, and Furry Family Team!

JUST LOOK AT US!!! WE WERE THE CUTEST BABIES!!!

Go across from left to right: HIPPY, VINNY, GATSBY, EMMA, CHARLIE, STELLA, FRANKIE, LOUIS, LOLA and Kekkei !!!

TRY TO RECOGNIZE US ON THE FOLLOWING PAGES!!! (Shh… The answers are on the last page.)

DAILY JOURNAL

LET THE ADVENTURE CONTINUE!

Date ___/___/20__

Sad moments…

_____

_____

Happy moments...

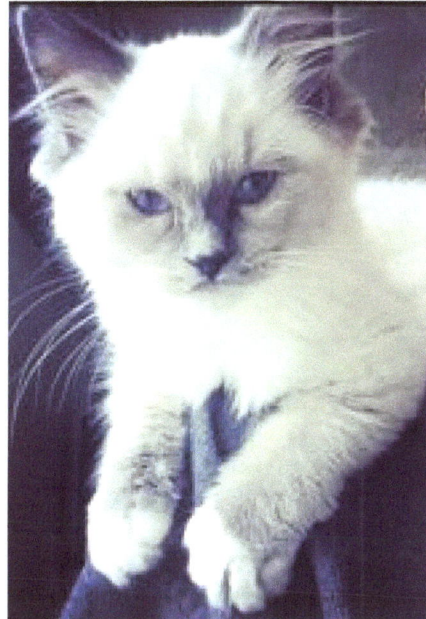

_____

_____

_____

Family Bonding Time…

- **WRITE OR DRAW SOMETHING FUNNY IN THE SPACE BELOW** THAT WILL PUT A HUGE SMILE ON YOUR FACE. ALWAYS TRY TO GO TO BED SMILING AND FEELING HAPPY!
- **THINK OF WAYS YOU CAN MAKE YOUR DAY EVEN BETTER TOMORROW. YOU CAN WRITE A TO DO LIST. THE DAY WILL GO MUCH SMOOTHER!**
- **ALWAYS SHARE** YOUR THOUGHTS AND CONCERNS WITH YOUR LOVING FAMILY FOR PROPER GUIDANCE AND GREAT IDEAS. WRITE THEM DOWN BELOW IF NEEDED.

Date ___/___/20__

Sad moments…

_____

_____

Happy moments...

_____

_____

_____

Family Bonding Time…

- **WRITE OR DRAW SOMETHING FUNNY IN THE SPACE BELOW** THAT WILL PUT A HUGE SMILE ON YOUR FACE. ALWAYS TRY TO GO TO BED SMILING AND FEELING HAPPY!
- **THINK OF WAYS** YOU CAN MAKE YOUR DAY EVEN BETTER TOMORROW. YOU CAN WRITE A TO DO LIST. THE DAY WILL GO MUCH SMOOTHER!
- **ALWAYS SHARE** YOUR THOUGHTS AND CONCERNS WITH YOUR LOVING FAMILY FOR PROPER GUIDANCE AND GREAT IDEAS. WRITE THEM DOWN BELOW IF NEEDED.

Date ___/___/20__

Sad moments…

_____

_____

Happy moments...

_____

_____

_____

Family Bonding Time…

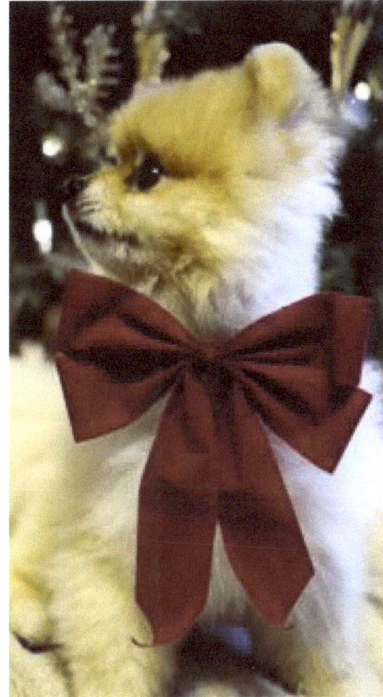

- **WRITE OR DRAW SOMETHING FUNNY IN THE SPACE BELOW** THAT WILL PUT A HUGE SMILE ON YOUR FACE. ALWAYS TRY TO GO TO BED SMILING AND FEELING HAPPY!
- **THINK OF WAYS YOU CAN MAKE YOUR DAY EVEN BETTER TOMORROW.** YOU CAN WRITE A TO DO LIST. THE DAY WILL GO MUCH SMOOTHER!
- **ALWAYS SHARE** YOUR THOUGHTS AND CONCERNS WITH YOUR LOVING FAMILY FOR PROPER GUIDANCE AND GREAT IDEAS. WRITE THEM DOWN BELOW IF NEEDED.

Date ___/___/20___

Sad moments…

_____

_____

Happy moments...

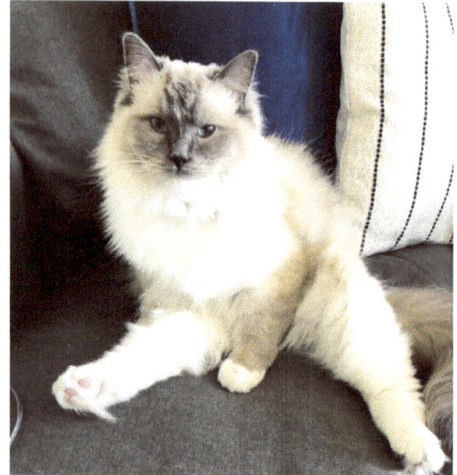

_____

_____

_____

Family Bonding Time…

- **WRITE OR DRAW SOMETHING FUNNY IN THE SPACE BELOW** THAT WILL PUT A HUGE SMILE ON YOUR FACE. ALWAYS TRY TO GO TO BED SMILING AND FEELING HAPPY!
- **THINK OF WAYS YOU CAN MAKE YOUR DAY EVEN BETTER TOMORROW.** YOU CAN WRITE A TO DO LIST. THE DAY WILL GO MUCH SMOOTHER!
- **ALWAYS SHARE** YOUR THOUGHTS AND CONCERNS WITH YOUR LOVING FAMILY FOR PROPER GUIDANCE AND GREAT IDEAS. WRITE THEM DOWN BELOW IF NEEDED.

Date ___/___/20__

Sad moments…

_____

_____

Happy moments...

_____

_____

_____

Family Bonding Time…

- **WRITE OR DRAW SOMETHING FUNNY IN THE SPACE BELOW** THAT WILL PUT A HUGE SMILE ON YOUR FACE. ALWAYS TRY TO GO TO BED SMILING AND FEELING HAPPY!
- **THINK OF WAYS YOU CAN MAKE YOUR DAY EVEN BETTER TOMORROW.** YOU CAN WRITE A TO DO LIST. THE DAY WILL GO MUCH SMOOTHER!
- **ALWAYS SHARE** YOUR THOUGHTS AND CONCERNS WITH YOUR LOVING FAMILY FOR PROPER GUIDANCE AND GREAT IDEAS. WRITE THEM DOWN BELOW IF NEEDED.

Date ___/___/20__

Sad moments…

_____

_____

Happy moments...

_____

_____

_____

Family Bonding Time…

- **WRITE OR DRAW SOMETHING FUNNY IN THE SPACE BELOW** THAT WILL PUT A HUGE SMILE ON YOUR FACE. ALWAYS TRY TO GO TO BED SMILING AND FEELING HAPPY!
- **THINK OF WAYS YOU CAN MAKE YOUR DAY EVEN BETTER TOMORROW. YOU CAN WRITE A TO DO LIST. THE DAY WILL GO MUCH SMOOTHER!**
- **ALWAYS SHARE** YOUR THOUGHTS AND CONCERNS WITH YOUR LOVING FAMILY FOR PROPER GUIDANCE AND GREAT IDEAS. WRITE THEM DOWN BELOW IF NEEDED.

Date ___/___/20__

Sad moments…

_____

_____

Happy moments...

_____

_____

_____

Family Bonding Time…

- **WRITE OR DRAW SOMETHING FUNNY IN THE SPACE BELOW** THAT WILL PUT A HUGE SMILE ON YOUR FACE. ALWAYS TRY TO GO TO BED SMILING AND FEELING HAPPY!
- **THINK OF WAYS YOU CAN MAKE YOUR DAY EVEN BETTER TOMORROW.** YOU CAN WRITE A TO DO LIST. THE DAY WILL GO MUCH SMOOTHER!
- **ALWAYS SHARE** YOUR THOUGHTS AND CONCERNS WITH YOUR LOVING FAMILY FOR PROPER GUIDANCE AND GREAT IDEAS. WRITE THEM DOWN BELOW IF NEEDED.

Date ___ / ___ /20__

Sad moments…

_____

_____

Happy moments...

_____

_____

_____

Family Bonding Time…

- **WRITE OR DRAW SOMETHING FUNNY IN THE SPACE BELOW** THAT WILL PUT A HUGE SMILE ON YOUR FACE. ALWAYS TRY TO GO TO BED SMILING AND FEELING HAPPY!
- **THINK OF WAYS YOU CAN MAKE YOUR DAY EVEN BETTER TOMORROW. YOU CAN WRITE A TO DO LIST. THE DAY WILL GO MUCH SMOOTHER!**
- **ALWAYS SHARE** YOUR THOUGHTS AND CONCERNS WITH YOUR LOVING FAMILY FOR PROPER GUIDANCE AND GREAT IDEAS. WRITE THEM DOWN BELOW IF NEEDED.

Date ___/___/20__

Sad moments…

_____

_____

Happy moments...

_____

_____

_____

Family Bonding Time…

- **WRITE OR DRAW SOMETHING FUNNY IN THE SPACE BELOW** THAT WILL PUT A HUGE SMILE ON YOUR FACE. ALWAYS TRY TO GO TO BED SMILING AND FEELING HAPPY!
- **THINK OF WAYS YOU CAN MAKE YOUR DAY EVEN BETTER TOMORROW.** YOU CAN WRITE A TO DO LIST. THE DAY WILL GO MUCH SMOOTHER!
- **ALWAYS SHARE** YOUR THOUGHTS AND CONCERNS WITH YOUR LOVING FAMILY FOR PROPER GUIDANCE AND GREAT IDEAS. WRITE THEM DOWN BELOW IF NEEDED.

Date ___/___/20__

Sad moments…

_____

_____

Happy moments...

_____

_____

_____

Family Bonding Time…

- **WRITE OR DRAW SOMETHING FUNNY IN THE SPACE BELOW** THAT WILL PUT A HUGE SMILE ON YOUR FACE. ALWAYS TRY TO GO TO BED SMILING AND FEELING HAPPY!
- **THINK OF WAYS YOU CAN MAKE YOUR DAY EVEN BETTER TOMORROW. YOU CAN WRITE A TO DO LIST. THE DAY WILL GO MUCH SMOOTHER!**
- **ALWAYS SHARE** YOUR THOUGHTS AND CONCERNS WITH YOUR LOVING FAMILY FOR PROPER GUIDANCE AND GREAT IDEAS. WRITE THEM DOWN BELOW IF NEEDED.

Date ___/___/20__

Sad moments…

_____

_____

Happy moments...

_____

_____

_____

Family Bonding Time…

- **WRITE OR DRAW SOMETHING FUNNY IN THE SPACE BELOW** THAT WILL PUT A HUGE SMILE ON YOUR FACE. ALWAYS TRY TO GO TO BED SMILING AND FEELING HAPPY!
- **THINK OF WAYS YOU CAN MAKE YOUR DAY EVEN BETTER TOMORROW. YOU CAN WRITE A TO DO LIST. THE DAY WILL GO MUCH SMOOTHER!**
- **ALWAYS SHARE** YOUR THOUGHTS AND CONCERNS WITH YOUR LOVING FAMILY FOR PROPER GUIDANCE AND GREAT IDEAS. WRITE THEM DOWN BELOW IF NEEDED.

Date ___/___/20__

Sad moments…

_____

_____

Happy moments...

_____

_____

_____

Family Bonding Time…

- **WRITE OR DRAW SOMETHING FUNNY IN THE SPACE BELOW** THAT WILL PUT A HUGE SMILE ON YOUR FACE. ALWAYS TRY TO GO TO BED SMILING AND FEELING HAPPY!
- **THINK OF WAYS YOU CAN MAKE YOUR DAY EVEN BETTER TOMORROW.** YOU CAN WRITE A TO DO LIST. THE DAY WILL GO MUCH SMOOTHER!
- **ALWAYS SHARE** YOUR THOUGHTS AND CONCERNS WITH YOUR LOVING FAMILY FOR PROPER GUIDANCE AND GREAT IDEAS. WRITE THEM DOWN BELOW IF NEEDED.

Date ___/___/20__

Sad moments…

_____

_____

Happy moments...

_____

_____

_____

Family Bonding Time…

- **WRITE OR DRAW SOMETHING FUNNY IN THE SPACE BELOW** THAT WILL PUT A HUGE SMILE ON YOUR FACE. ALWAYS TRY TO GO TO BED SMILING AND FEELING HAPPY!
- **THINK OF WAYS YOU CAN MAKE YOUR DAY EVEN BETTER TOMORROW.** YOU CAN WRITE A TO DO LIST. THE DAY WILL GO MUCH SMOOTHER!
- **ALWAYS SHARE** YOUR THOUGHTS AND CONCERNS WITH YOUR LOVING FAMILY FOR PROPER GUIDANCE AND GREAT IDEAS. WRITE THEM DOWN BELOW IF NEEDED.

Date ___/___/20__

Sad moments…

_____

_____

Happy moments...

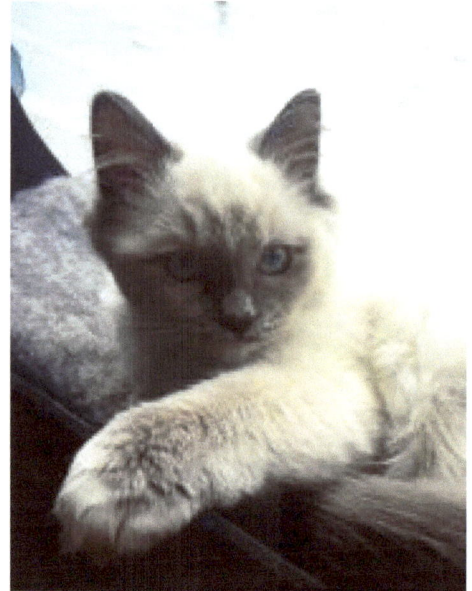

_____

_____

_____

Family Bonding Time…

- **WRITE OR DRAW SOMETHING FUNNY IN THE SPACE BELOW** THAT WILL PUT A HUGE SMILE ON YOUR FACE. ALWAYS TRY TO GO TO BED SMILING AND FEELING HAPPY!
- **THINK OF WAYS YOU CAN MAKE YOUR DAY EVEN BETTER TOMORROW. YOU CAN WRITE A TO DO LIST. THE DAY WILL GO MUCH SMOOTHER!**
- **ALWAYS SHARE** YOUR THOUGHTS AND CONCERNS WITH YOUR LOVING FAMILY FOR PROPER GUIDANCE AND GREAT IDEAS. WRITE THEM DOWN BELOW IF NEEDED.

Date ___/___/20__

Sad moments…

_____

_____

Happy moments...

_____

_____

_____

Family Bonding Time…

- **WRITE OR DRAW SOMETHING FUNNY IN THE SPACE BELOW** THAT WILL PUT A HUGE SMILE ON YOUR FACE. ALWAYS TRY TO GO TO BED SMILING AND FEELING HAPPY!
- **THINK OF WAYS YOU CAN MAKE YOUR DAY EVEN BETTER TOMORROW.** YOU CAN WRITE A TO DO LIST. THE DAY WILL GO MUCH SMOOTHER!
- **ALWAYS SHARE** YOUR THOUGHTS AND CONCERNS WITH YOUR LOVING FAMILY FOR PROPER GUIDANCE AND GREAT IDEAS. WRITE THEM DOWN BELOW IF NEEDED.

Date ___/___/20__

Sad moments…

_____

_____

Happy moments...

_____

_____

_____

Family Bonding Time…

- **WRITE OR DRAW SOMETHING FUNNY IN THE SPACE BELOW** THAT WILL PUT A HUGE SMILE ON YOUR FACE. ALWAYS TRY TO GO TO BED SMILING AND FEELING HAPPY!
- **THINK OF WAYS YOU CAN MAKE YOUR DAY EVEN BETTER TOMORROW.** YOU CAN WRITE A TO DO LIST. THE DAY WILL GO MUCH SMOOTHER!
- **ALWAYS SHARE** YOUR THOUGHTS AND CONCERNS WITH YOUR LOVING FAMILY FOR PROPER GUIDANCE AND GREAT IDEAS. WRITE THEM DOWN BELOW IF NEEDED.

Date ___/___/20__

Sad moments...

_____

_____

Happy moments...

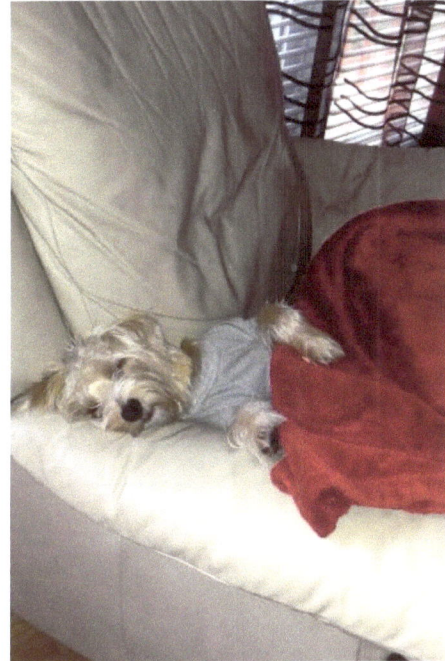

_____

_____

_____

Family Bonding Time...

- **WRITE OR DRAW SOMETHING FUNNY IN THE SPACE BELOW** THAT WILL PUT A HUGE SMILE ON YOUR FACE. ALWAYS TRY TO GO TO BED SMILING AND FEELING HAPPY!

- **THINK OF WAYS YOU CAN MAKE YOUR DAY EVEN BETTER TOMORROW.** YOU CAN WRITE A TO DO LIST. THE DAY WILL GO MUCH SMOOTHER!

- **ALWAYS SHARE** YOUR THOUGHTS AND CONCERNS WITH YOUR LOVING FAMILY FOR PROPER GUIDANCE AND GREAT IDEAS. WRITE THEM DOWN BELOW IF NEEDED.

Date ___/___/20__

Sad moments…

_____

_____

Happy moments...

_____

_____

_____

Family Bonding Time…

- **WRITE OR DRAW SOMETHING FUNNY IN THE SPACE BELOW** THAT WILL PUT A HUGE SMILE ON YOUR FACE. ALWAYS TRY TO GO TO BED SMILING AND FEELING HAPPY!
- **THINK OF WAYS YOU CAN MAKE YOUR DAY EVEN BETTER TOMORROW.** YOU CAN WRITE A TO DO LIST. THE DAY WILL GO MUCH SMOOTHER!
- **ALWAYS SHARE** YOUR THOUGHTS AND CONCERNS WITH YOUR LOVING FAMILY FOR PROPER GUIDANCE AND GREAT IDEAS. WRITE THEM DOWN BELOW IF NEEDED.

Date ___/___/20__

Sad moments…

_____

_____

Happy moments...

_____

_____

_____

Family Bonding Time…

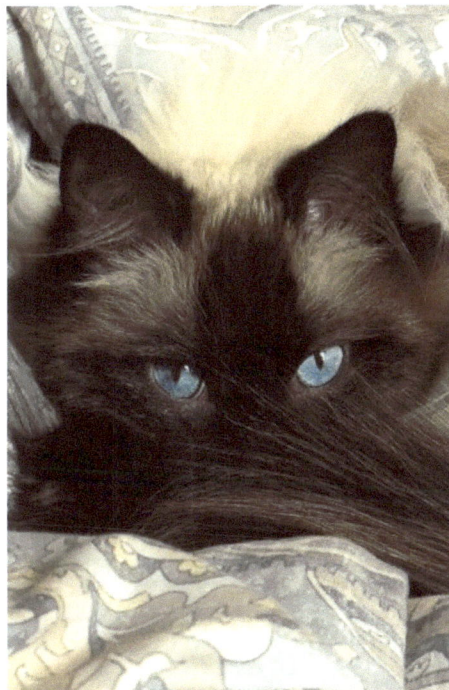

- **WRITE OR DRAW SOMETHING FUNNY IN THE SPACE BELOW** THAT WILL PUT A HUGE SMILE ON YOUR FACE. ALWAYS TRY TO GO TO BED SMILING AND FEELING HAPPY!
- **THINK OF WAYS YOU CAN MAKE YOUR DAY EVEN BETTER TOMORROW.** YOU CAN WRITE A TO DO LIST. THE DAY WILL GO MUCH SMOOTHER!
- **ALWAYS SHARE** YOUR THOUGHTS AND CONCERNS WITH YOUR LOVING FAMILY FOR PROPER GUIDANCE AND GREAT IDEAS. WRITE THEM DOWN BELOW IF NEEDED.

Date ___/___/20__

Sad moments…

_____

_____

Happy moments...

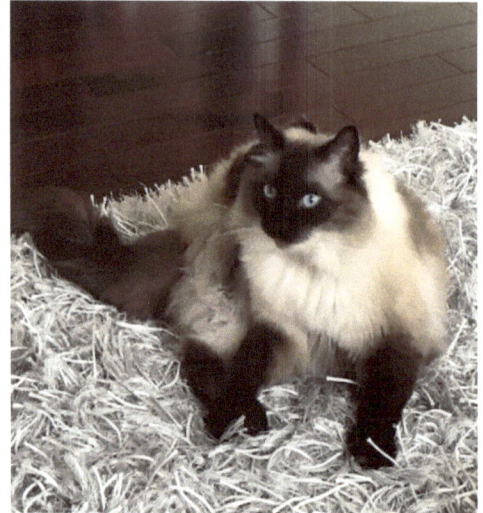

_____

_____

_____

Family Bonding Time…

- WRITE OR DRAW SOMETHING FUNNY IN THE SPACE BELOW THAT WILL PUT A HUGE SMILE ON YOUR FACE. ALWAYS TRY TO GO TO BED SMILING AND FEELING HAPPY!
- THINK OF WAYS YOU CAN MAKE YOUR DAY EVEN BETTER TOMORROW. YOU CAN WRITE A TO DO LIST. THE DAY WILL GO MUCH SMOOTHER!
- ALWAYS SHARE YOUR THOUGHTS AND CONCERNS WITH YOUR LOVING FAMILY FOR PROPER GUIDANCE AND GREAT IDEAS. WRITE THEM DOWN BELOW IF NEEDED.

Date ___/___/20__

Sad moments…

_____

_____

Happy moments...

_____

_____

_____

Family Bonding Time…

- **WRITE OR DRAW SOMETHING FUNNY IN THE SPACE BELOW** THAT WILL PUT A HUGE SMILE ON YOUR FACE. ALWAYS TRY TO GO TO BED SMILING AND FEELING HAPPY!
- **THINK OF WAYS YOU CAN MAKE YOUR DAY EVEN BETTER TOMORROW.** YOU CAN WRITE A TO DO LIST. THE DAY WILL GO MUCH SMOOTHER!
- **ALWAYS SHARE** YOUR THOUGHTS AND CONCERNS WITH YOUR LOVING FAMILY FOR PROPER GUIDANCE AND GREAT IDEAS. WRITE THEM DOWN BELOW IF NEEDED.

Date ___/___/20__

Sad moments…

_____

_____

Happy moments...

_____

_____

_____

Family Bonding Time…

- **WRITE OR DRAW SOMETHING FUNNY IN THE SPACE BELOW** THAT WILL PUT A HUGE SMILE ON YOUR FACE. ALWAYS TRY TO GO TO BED SMILING AND FEELING HAPPY!
- **THINK OF WAYS YOU CAN MAKE YOUR DAY EVEN BETTER TOMORROW. YOU CAN WRITE A TO DO LIST. THE DAY WILL GO MUCH SMOOTHER!**
- **ALWAYS SHARE** YOUR THOUGHTS AND CONCERNS WITH YOUR LOVING FAMILY FOR PROPER GUIDANCE AND GREAT IDEAS. WRITE THEM DOWN BELOW IF NEEDED.

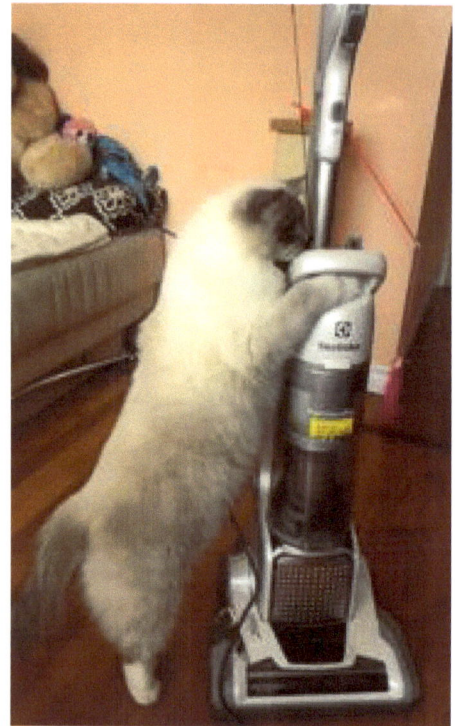

Date ___/___/20__

Sad moments…

_____

_____

Happy moments...

_____

_____

_____

Family Bonding Time…

- **WRITE OR DRAW SOMETHING FUNNY IN THE SPACE BELOW** THAT WILL PUT A HUGE SMILE ON YOUR FACE. ALWAYS TRY TO GO TO BED SMILING AND FEELING HAPPY!
- **THINK OF WAYS YOU CAN MAKE YOUR DAY EVEN BETTER TOMORROW. YOU CAN WRITE A TO DO LIST. THE DAY WILL GO MUCH SMOOTHER!**
- **ALWAYS SHARE** YOUR THOUGHTS AND CONCERNS WITH YOUR LOVING FAMILY FOR PROPER GUIDANCE AND GREAT IDEAS. WRITE THEM DOWN BELOW IF NEEDED.

Date ___/___/20__

Sad moments…

_____

_____

Happy moments...

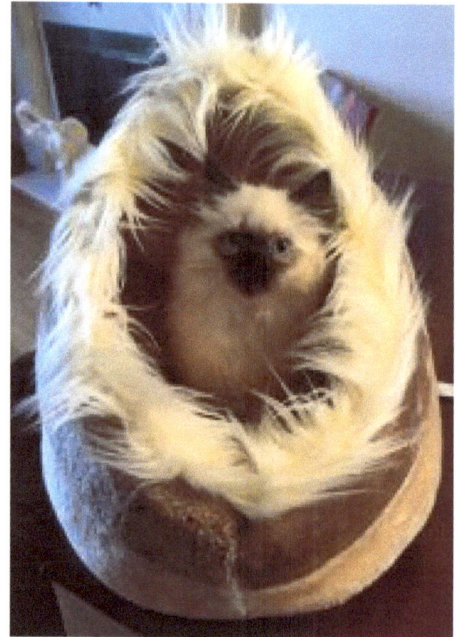

_____

_____

_____

Family Bonding Time…

- **WRITE OR DRAW SOMETHING FUNNY IN THE SPACE BELOW** THAT WILL PUT A HUGE SMILE ON YOUR FACE. ALWAYS TRY TO GO TO BED SMILING AND FEELING HAPPY!
- **THINK OF WAYS YOU CAN MAKE YOUR DAY EVEN BETTER TOMORROW. YOU CAN WRITE A TO DO LIST. THE DAY WILL GO MUCH SMOOTHER!**
- **ALWAYS SHARE** YOUR THOUGHTS AND CONCERNS WITH YOUR LOVING FAMILY FOR PROPER GUIDANCE AND GREAT IDEAS. WRITE THEM DOWN BELOW IF NEEDED.

Date ___/___/20__

Sad moments…

_____

_____

Happy moments...

_____

_____

_____

Family Bonding Time…

- **WRITE OR DRAW SOMETHING FUNNY IN THE SPACE BELOW** THAT WILL PUT A HUGE SMILE ON YOUR FACE. ALWAYS TRY TO GO TO BED SMILING AND FEELING HAPPY!
- **THINK OF WAYS YOU CAN MAKE YOUR DAY EVEN BETTER TOMORROW. YOU CAN WRITE A TO DO LIST. THE DAY WILL GO MUCH SMOOTHER!**
- **ALWAYS SHARE** YOUR THOUGHTS AND CONCERNS WITH YOUR LOVING FAMILY FOR PROPER GUIDANCE AND GREAT IDEAS. WRITE THEM DOWN BELOW IF NEEDED.

Date ___/___/20__

Sad moments…

_____

_____

Happy moments...

_____

_____

_____

Family Bonding Time…

- **WRITE OR DRAW SOMETHING FUNNY IN THE SPACE BELOW** THAT WILL PUT A HUGE SMILE ON YOUR FACE. ALWAYS TRY TO GO TO BED SMILING AND FEELING HAPPY!

- **THINK OF WAYS YOU CAN MAKE YOUR DAY EVEN BETTER TOMORROW. YOU CAN WRITE A TO DO LIST. THE DAY WILL GO MUCH SMOOTHER!**

- **ALWAYS SHARE** YOUR THOUGHTS AND CONCERNS WITH YOUR LOVING FAMILY FOR PROPER GUIDANCE AND GREAT IDEAS. WRITE THEM DOWN BELOW IF NEEDED.

Date ___/___/20__

Sad moments…

_____

_____

Happy moments...

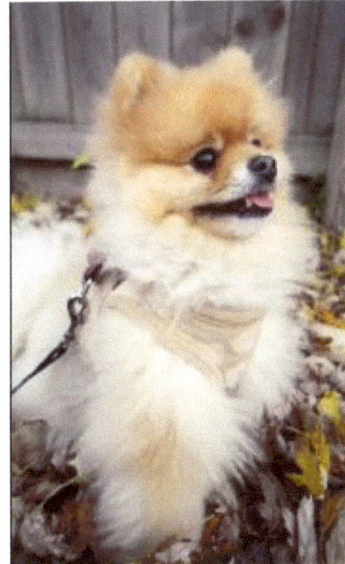

_____

_____

_____

Family Bonding Time…

- **WRITE OR DRAW SOMETHING FUNNY IN THE SPACE BELOW** THAT WILL PUT A HUGE SMILE ON YOUR FACE. ALWAYS TRY TO GO TO BED SMILING AND FEELING HAPPY!
- **THINK OF WAYS YOU CAN MAKE YOUR DAY EVEN BETTER TOMORROW. YOU CAN WRITE A TO DO LIST. THE DAY WILL GO MUCH SMOOTHER!**
- **ALWAYS SHARE** YOUR THOUGHTS AND CONCERNS WITH YOUR LOVING FAMILY FOR PROPER GUIDANCE AND GREAT IDEAS. WRITE THEM DOWN BELOW IF NEEDED.

Date ___/___/20__

Sad moments…

_____

_____

Happy moments...

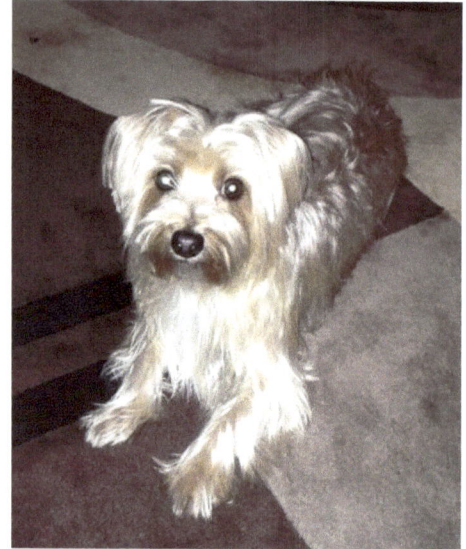

_____

_____

_____

Family Bonding Time…

- WRITE OR DRAW SOMETHING FUNNY IN THE SPACE BELOW THAT WILL PUT A HUGE SMILE ON YOUR FACE. ALWAYS TRY TO GO TO BED SMILING AND FEELING HAPPY!
- THINK OF WAYS YOU CAN MAKE YOUR DAY EVEN BETTER TOMORROW. YOU CAN WRITE A TO DO LIST. THE DAY WILL GO MUCH SMOOTHER!
- ALWAYS SHARE YOUR THOUGHTS AND CONCERNS WITH YOUR LOVING FAMILY FOR PROPER GUIDANCE AND GREAT IDEAS. WRITE THEM DOWN BELOW IF NEEDED.

Date ___/___/20__

Sad moments…

_____

_____

Happy moments...

_____

_____

_____

Family Bonding Time…

- **WRITE OR DRAW SOMETHING FUNNY IN THE SPACE BELOW** THAT WILL PUT A HUGE SMILE ON YOUR FACE. ALWAYS TRY TO GO TO BED SMILING AND FEELING HAPPY!
- **THINK OF WAYS YOU CAN MAKE YOUR DAY EVEN BETTER TOMORROW.** YOU CAN WRITE A TO DO LIST. THE DAY WILL GO MUCH SMOOTHER!
- **ALWAYS SHARE** YOUR THOUGHTS AND CONCERNS WITH YOUR LOVING FAMILY FOR PROPER GUIDANCE AND GREAT IDEAS. WRITE THEM DOWN BELOW IF NEEDED.

Date ___/___/20__

Sad moments…

_____

_____

Happy moments...

_____

_____

_____

Family Bonding Time…

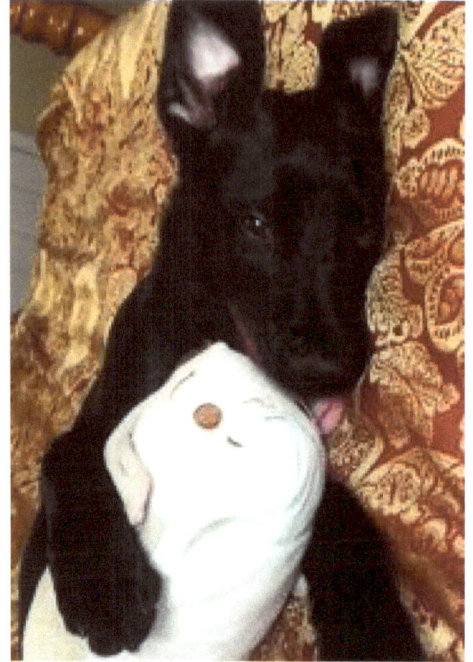

- **WRITE OR DRAW SOMETHING FUNNY IN THE SPACE BELOW** THAT WILL PUT A HUGE SMILE ON YOUR FACE. ALWAYS TRY TO GO TO BED SMILING AND FEELING HAPPY!
- **THINK OF WAYS** YOU CAN MAKE YOUR DAY EVEN BETTER TOMORROW. YOU CAN WRITE A TO DO LIST. THE DAY WILL GO MUCH SMOOTHER!
- **ALWAYS SHARE** YOUR THOUGHTS AND CONCERNS WITH YOUR LOVING FAMILY FOR PROPER GUIDANCE AND GREAT IDEAS. WRITE THEM DOWN BELOW IF NEEDED.

Date ___/___/20__

Sad moments...

_____

_____

Happy moments...

_____

_____

_____

Family Bonding Time...

- **WRITE OR DRAW SOMETHING FUNNY IN THE SPACE BELOW** THAT WILL PUT A HUGE SMILE ON YOUR FACE. ALWAYS TRY TO GO TO BED SMILING AND FEELING HAPPY!
- **THINK OF WAYS YOU CAN MAKE YOUR DAY EVEN BETTER TOMORROW. YOU CAN WRITE A TO DO LIST. THE DAY WILL GO MUCH SMOOTHER!**
- **ALWAYS SHARE** YOUR THOUGHTS AND CONCERNS WITH YOUR LOVING FAMILY FOR PROPER GUIDANCE AND GREAT IDEAS. WRITE THEM DOWN BELOW IF NEEDED.

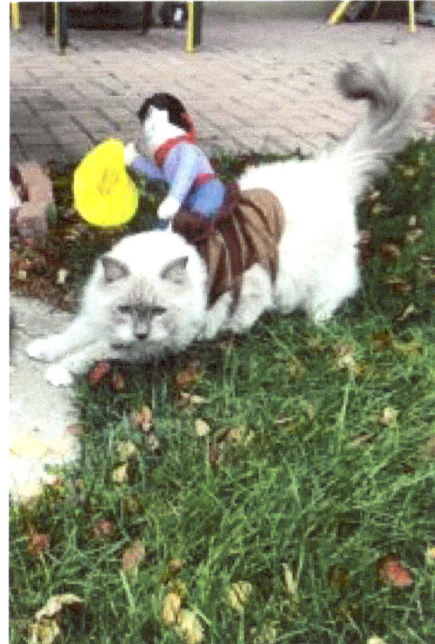

Date ___/___/20__

Sad moments…

_____

_____

Happy moments...

_____

_____

_____

Family Bonding Time…

- **WRITE OR DRAW SOMETHING FUNNY IN THE SPACE BELOW** THAT WILL PUT A HUGE SMILE ON YOUR FACE. ALWAYS TRY TO GO TO BED SMILING AND FEELING HAPPY!
- **THINK OF WAYS YOU CAN MAKE YOUR DAY EVEN BETTER TOMORROW. YOU CAN WRITE A TO DO LIST. THE DAY WILL GO MUCH SMOOTHER!**
- **ALWAYS SHARE** YOUR THOUGHTS AND CONCERNS WITH YOUR LOVING FAMILY FOR PROPER GUIDANCE AND GREAT IDEAS. WRITE THEM DOWN BELOW IF NEEDED.

Date ___/___/20__

Sad moments…

_____

_____

Happy moments...

_____

_____

_____

Family Bonding Time…

- **WRITE OR DRAW SOMETHING FUNNY IN THE SPACE BELOW** THAT WILL PUT A HUGE SMILE ON YOUR FACE. ALWAYS TRY TO GO TO BED SMILING AND FEELING HAPPY!
- **THINK OF WAYS YOU CAN MAKE YOUR DAY EVEN BETTER TOMORROW.** YOU CAN WRITE A TO DO LIST. THE DAY WILL GO MUCH SMOOTHER!
- **ALWAYS SHARE** YOUR THOUGHTS AND CONCERNS WITH YOUR LOVING FAMILY FOR PROPER GUIDANCE AND GREAT IDEAS. WRITE THEM DOWN BELOW IF NEEDED.

Date ___/___/20__

Sad moments…

_____

_____

Happy moments…

_____

_____

_____

Family Bonding Time…

- **WRITE OR DRAW SOMETHING FUNNY IN THE SPACE BELOW** THAT WILL PUT A HUGE SMILE ON YOUR FACE. ALWAYS TRY TO GO TO BED SMILING AND FEELING HAPPY!
- **THINK OF WAYS YOU CAN MAKE YOUR DAY EVEN BETTER TOMORROW. YOU CAN WRITE A TO DO LIST. THE DAY WILL GO MUCH SMOOTHER!**
- **ALWAYS SHARE** YOUR THOUGHTS AND CONCERNS WITH YOUR LOVING FAMILY FOR PROPER GUIDANCE AND GREAT IDEAS. WRITE THEM DOWN BELOW IF NEEDED.

Date ___/___/20__

Sad moments…

_____

_____

Happy moments...

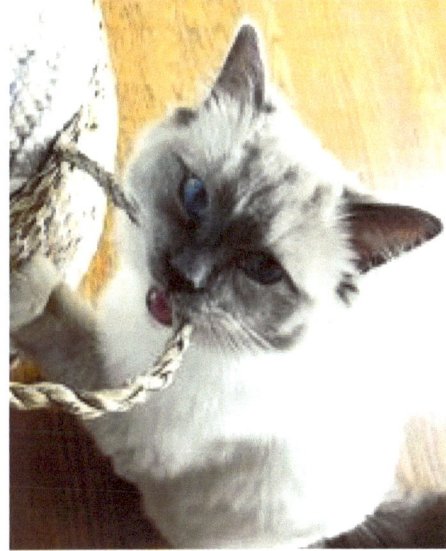

_____

_____

_____

Family Bonding Time…

- **WRITE OR DRAW SOMETHING FUNNY IN THE SPACE BELOW** THAT WILL PUT A HUGE SMILE ON YOUR FACE. ALWAYS TRY TO GO TO BED SMILING AND FEELING HAPPY!
- **THINK OF WAYS YOU CAN MAKE YOUR DAY EVEN BETTER TOMORROW. YOU CAN WRITE A TO DO LIST. THE DAY WILL GO MUCH SMOOTHER!**
- **ALWAYS SHARE** YOUR THOUGHTS AND CONCERNS WITH YOUR LOVING FAMILY FOR PROPER GUIDANCE AND GREAT IDEAS. WRITE THEM DOWN BELOW IF NEEDED.

Date ___/___/20__

Sad moments...

_____

_____

Happy moments...

_____

_____

_____

Family Bonding Time...

- **WRITE OR DRAW SOMETHING FUNNY IN THE SPACE BELOW** THAT WILL PUT A HUGE SMILE ON YOUR FACE. ALWAYS TRY TO GO TO BED SMILING AND FEELING HAPPY!
- **THINK OF WAYS YOU CAN MAKE YOUR DAY EVEN BETTER TOMORROW. YOU CAN WRITE A TO DO LIST. THE DAY WILL GO MUCH SMOOTHER!**
- **ALWAYS SHARE** YOUR THOUGHTS AND CONCERNS WITH YOUR LOVING FAMILY FOR PROPER GUIDANCE AND GREAT IDEAS. WRITE THEM DOWN BELOW IF NEEDED.

Date ___/___/20__

Sad moments…

_____

_____

Happy moments...

_____

_____

_____

Family Bonding Time…

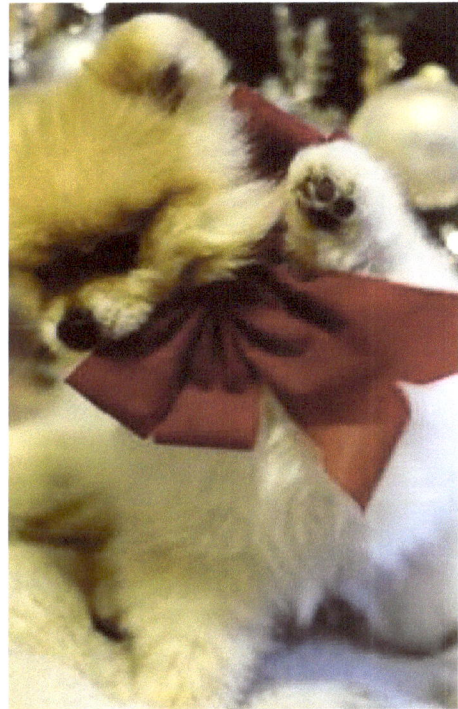

- **WRITE OR DRAW SOMETHING FUNNY IN THE SPACE BELOW** THAT WILL PUT A HUGE SMILE ON YOUR FACE. ALWAYS TRY TO GO TO BED SMILING AND FEELING HAPPY!
- **THINK OF WAYS YOU CAN MAKE YOUR DAY EVEN BETTER TOMORROW.** YOU CAN WRITE A TO DO LIST. THE DAY WILL GO MUCH SMOOTHER!
- **ALWAYS SHARE** YOUR THOUGHTS AND CONCERNS WITH YOUR LOVING FAMILY FOR PROPER GUIDANCE AND GREAT IDEAS. WRITE THEM DOWN BELOW IF NEEDED.

Date ___/___/20__

Sad moments…

_____

_____

Happy moments...

_____

_____

_____

Family Bonding Time…

- **WRITE OR DRAW SOMETHING FUNNY IN THE SPACE BELOW** THAT WILL PUT A HUGE SMILE ON YOUR FACE. ALWAYS TRY TO GO TO BED SMILING AND FEELING HAPPY!
- **THINK OF WAYS YOU CAN MAKE YOUR DAY EVEN BETTER TOMORROW. YOU CAN WRITE A TO DO LIST. THE DAY WILL GO MUCH SMOOTHER!**
- **ALWAYS SHARE** YOUR THOUGHTS AND CONCERNS WITH YOUR LOVING FAMILY FOR PROPER GUIDANCE AND GREAT IDEAS. WRITE THEM DOWN BELOW IF NEEDED.

Date ___/___/20__

Sad moments…

_____

_____

Happy moments...

_____

_____

_____

Family Bonding Time…

- **WRITE OR DRAW SOMETHING FUNNY IN THE SPACE BELOW** THAT WILL PUT A HUGE SMILE ON YOUR FACE. ALWAYS TRY TO GO TO BED SMILING AND FEELING HAPPY!
- **THINK OF WAYS YOU CAN MAKE YOUR DAY EVEN BETTER TOMORROW.** YOU CAN WRITE A TO DO LIST. THE DAY WILL GO MUCH SMOOTHER!
- **ALWAYS SHARE** YOUR THOUGHTS AND CONCERNS WITH YOUR LOVING FAMILY FOR PROPER GUIDANCE AND GREAT IDEAS. WRITE THEM DOWN BELOW IF NEEDED.

Date ___/___/20__

Sad moments...

_____

_____

Happy moments...

_____

_____

_____

Family Bonding Time...

- **WRITE OR DRAW SOMETHING FUNNY IN THE SPACE BELOW** THAT WILL PUT A HUGE SMILE ON YOUR FACE. ALWAYS TRY TO GO TO BED SMILING AND FEELING HAPPY!
- **THINK OF WAYS YOU CAN MAKE YOUR DAY EVEN BETTER TOMORROW. YOU CAN WRITE A TO DO LIST. THE DAY WILL GO MUCH SMOOTHER!**
- **ALWAYS SHARE** YOUR THOUGHTS AND CONCERNS WITH YOUR LOVING FAMILY FOR PROPER GUIDANCE AND GREAT IDEAS. WRITE THEM DOWN BELOW IF NEEDED.

Date ___/___/20__

Sad moments…

_____

_____

Happy moments...

_____

_____

_____

Family Bonding Time…

- **WRITE OR DRAW SOMETHING FUNNY IN THE SPACE BELOW** THAT WILL PUT A HUGE SMILE ON YOUR FACE. ALWAYS TRY TO GO TO BED SMILING AND FEELING HAPPY!
- **THINK OF WAYS YOU CAN MAKE YOUR DAY EVEN BETTER TOMORROW. YOU CAN WRITE A TO DO LIST. THE DAY WILL GO MUCH SMOOTHER!**
- **ALWAYS SHARE** YOUR THOUGHTS AND CONCERNS WITH YOUR LOVING FAMILY FOR PROPER GUIDANCE AND GREAT IDEAS. WRITE THEM DOWN BELOW IF NEEDED.

Date ___/___/20__

Sad moments...

_____

_____

Happy moments...

_____

_____

_____

Family Bonding Time...

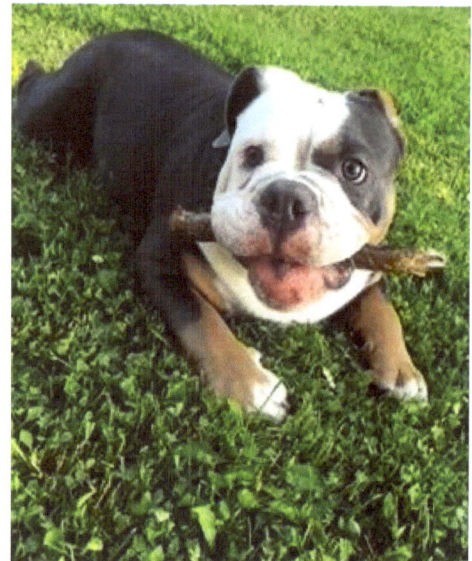

- **WRITE OR DRAW SOMETHING FUNNY IN THE SPACE BELOW** THAT WILL PUT A HUGE SMILE ON YOUR FACE. ALWAYS TRY TO GO TO BED SMILING AND FEELING HAPPY!
- **THINK OF WAYS YOU CAN MAKE YOUR DAY EVEN BETTER TOMORROW. YOU CAN WRITE A TO DO LIST. THE DAY WILL GO MUCH SMOOTHER!**
- **ALWAYS SHARE** YOUR THOUGHTS AND CONCERNS WITH YOUR LOVING FAMILY FOR PROPER GUIDANCE AND GREAT IDEAS. WRITE THEM DOWN BELOW IF NEEDED.

Date ___/___/20__

Sad moments…

_____

_____

Happy moments...

_____

_____

_____

Family Bonding Time…

- **WRITE OR DRAW SOMETHING FUNNY IN THE SPACE BELOW** THAT WILL PUT A HUGE SMILE ON YOUR FACE. ALWAYS TRY TO GO TO BED SMILING AND FEELING HAPPY!
- **THINK OF WAYS YOU CAN MAKE YOUR DAY EVEN BETTER TOMORROW. YOU CAN WRITE A TO DO LIST. THE DAY WILL GO MUCH SMOOTHER!**
- **ALWAYS SHARE** YOUR THOUGHTS AND CONCERNS WITH YOUR LOVING FAMILY FOR PROPER GUIDANCE AND GREAT IDEAS. WRITE THEM DOWN BELOW IF NEEDED.

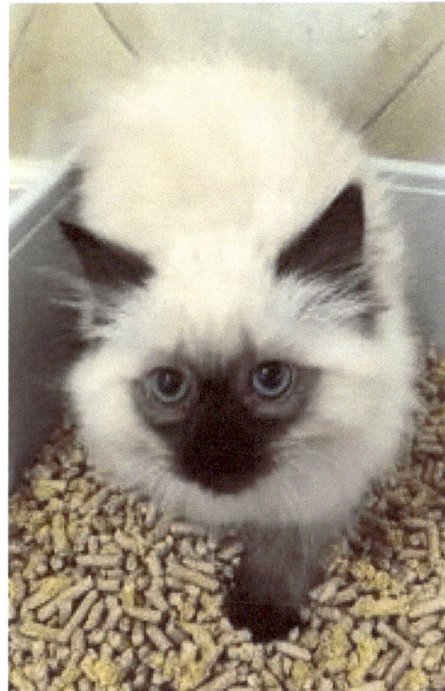

Date ___/___/20__

Sad moments...

_____

_____

Happy moments...

_____

_____

_____

Family Bonding Time...

- **WRITE OR DRAW SOMETHING FUNNY IN THE SPACE BELOW** THAT WILL PUT A HUGE SMILE ON YOUR FACE. ALWAYS TRY TO GO TO BED SMILING AND FEELING HAPPY!
- **THINK OF WAYS YOU CAN MAKE YOUR DAY EVEN BETTER TOMORROW. YOU CAN WRITE A TO DO LIST. THE DAY WILL GO MUCH SMOOTHER!**
- **ALWAYS SHARE** YOUR THOUGHTS AND CONCERNS WITH YOUR LOVING FAMILY FOR PROPER GUIDANCE AND GREAT IDEAS. WRITE THEM DOWN BELOW IF NEEDED.

Date ___/___/20__

Sad moments…

_____

_____

Happy moments...

_____

_____

_____

Family Bonding Time…

- **WRITE OR DRAW SOMETHING FUNNY IN THE SPACE BELOW** THAT WILL PUT A HUGE SMILE ON YOUR FACE. ALWAYS TRY TO GO TO BED SMILING AND FEELING HAPPY!
- **THINK OF WAYS YOU CAN MAKE YOUR DAY EVEN BETTER TOMORROW. YOU CAN WRITE A TO DO LIST. THE DAY WILL GO MUCH SMOOTHER!**
- **ALWAYS SHARE** YOUR THOUGHTS AND CONCERNS WITH YOUR LOVING FAMILY FOR PROPER GUIDANCE AND GREAT IDEAS. WRITE THEM DOWN BELOW IF NEEDED.

Date ___/___/20__

Sad moments…

_____

_____

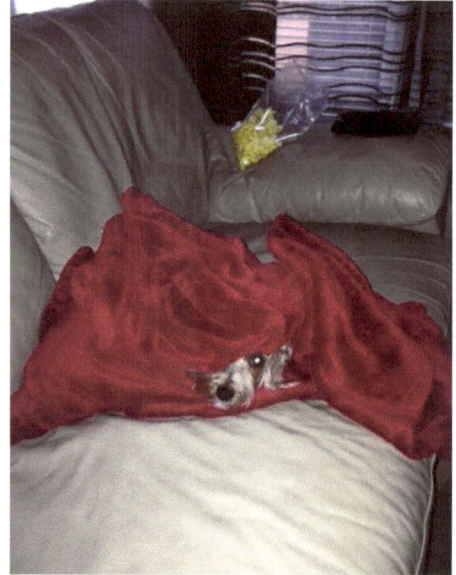

Happy moments...

_____

_____

_____

Family Bonding Time…

- **WRITE OR DRAW SOMETHING FUNNY IN THE SPACE BELOW** THAT WILL PUT A HUGE SMILE ON YOUR FACE. ALWAYS TRY TO GO TO BED SMILING AND FEELING HAPPY!
- **THINK OF WAYS YOU CAN MAKE YOUR DAY EVEN BETTER TOMORROW. YOU CAN WRITE A TO DO LIST. THE DAY WILL GO MUCH SMOOTHER!**
- **ALWAYS SHARE** YOUR THOUGHTS AND CONCERNS WITH YOUR LOVING FAMILY FOR PROPER GUIDANCE AND GREAT IDEAS. WRITE THEM DOWN BELOW IF NEEDED.

Date ___/___/20__

Sad moments…

_____

_____

Happy moments...

_____

_____

_____

Family Bonding Time…

- **WRITE OR DRAW SOMETHING FUNNY IN THE SPACE BELOW** THAT WILL PUT A HUGE SMILE ON YOUR FACE. ALWAYS TRY TO GO TO BED SMILING AND FEELING HAPPY!
- **THINK OF WAYS YOU CAN MAKE YOUR DAY EVEN BETTER TOMORROW.** YOU CAN WRITE A TO DO LIST. THE DAY WILL GO MUCH SMOOTHER!
- **ALWAYS SHARE** YOUR THOUGHTS AND CONCERNS WITH YOUR LOVING FAMILY FOR PROPER GUIDANCE AND GREAT IDEAS. WRITE THEM DOWN BELOW IF NEEDED.

Date ___/___/20__

Sad moments...

_____

_____

Happy moments...

_____

_____

_____

Family Bonding Time...

- **WRITE OR DRAW SOMETHING FUNNY IN THE SPACE BELOW** THAT WILL PUT A HUGE SMILE ON YOUR FACE. ALWAYS TRY TO GO TO BED SMILING AND FEELING HAPPY!
- **THINK OF WAYS YOU CAN MAKE YOUR DAY EVEN BETTER TOMORROW. YOU CAN WRITE A TO DO LIST. THE DAY WILL GO MUCH SMOOTHER!**
- **ALWAYS SHARE** YOUR THOUGHTS AND CONCERNS WITH YOUR LOVING FAMILY FOR PROPER GUIDANCE AND GREAT IDEAS. WRITE THEM DOWN BELOW IF NEEDED.

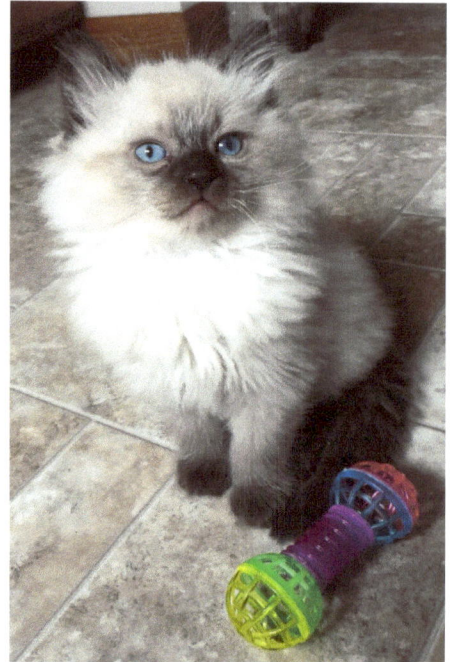

Date ___/___/20__

Sad moments…

_____

_____

Happy moments...

_____

_____

_____

Family Bonding Time…

- **WRITE OR DRAW SOMETHING FUNNY IN THE SPACE BELOW** THAT WILL PUT A HUGE SMILE ON YOUR FACE. ALWAYS TRY TO GO TO BED SMILING AND FEELING HAPPY!
- **THINK OF WAYS YOU CAN MAKE YOUR DAY EVEN BETTER TOMORROW.** YOU CAN WRITE A TO DO LIST. THE DAY WILL GO MUCH SMOOTHER!
- **ALWAYS SHARE** YOUR THOUGHTS AND CONCERNS WITH YOUR LOVING FAMILY FOR PROPER GUIDANCE AND GREAT IDEAS. WRITE THEM DOWN BELOW IF NEEDED.

Date ___/___/20__

Sad moments...

_____

_____

Happy moments...

_____

_____

_____

Family Bonding Time...

- **WRITE OR DRAW SOMETHING FUNNY IN THE SPACE BELOW** THAT WILL PUT A HUGE SMILE ON YOUR FACE. ALWAYS TRY TO GO TO BED SMILING AND FEELING HAPPY!
- **THINK OF WAYS** YOU CAN MAKE YOUR DAY EVEN BETTER TOMORROW. YOU CAN WRITE A TO DO LIST. THE DAY WILL GO MUCH SMOOTHER!
- **ALWAYS SHARE** YOUR THOUGHTS AND CONCERNS WITH YOUR LOVING FAMILY FOR PROPER GUIDANCE AND GREAT IDEAS. WRITE THEM DOWN BELOW IF NEEDED.

Date ___/___/20__

Sad moments…

_____

_____

Happy moments...

_____

_____

_____

Family Bonding Time…

- WRITE OR DRAW SOMETHING FUNNY IN THE SPACE BELOW THAT WILL PUT A
HUGE SMILE ON YOUR FACE. ALWAYS TRY TO GO TO BED SMILING AND FEELING
HAPPY!
- THINK OF WAYS YOU CAN MAKE YOUR DAY EVEN BETTER TOMORROW. YOU
CAN WRITE A TO DO LIST. THE DAY WILL GO MUCH SMOOTHER!
- ALWAYS SHARE YOUR THOUGHTS AND CONCERNS WITH YOUR LOVING FAMILY
FOR PROPER GUIDANCE AND GREAT IDEAS. WRITE THEM DOWN BELOW IF NEEDED.

Date ___/___/20__

Sad moments...

_____

_____

Happy moments...

_____

_____

_____

Family Bonding Time...

- **WRITE OR DRAW SOMETHING FUNNY IN THE SPACE BELOW** THAT WILL PUT A HUGE SMILE ON YOUR FACE. ALWAYS TRY TO GO TO BED SMILING AND FEELING HAPPY!
- **THINK OF WAYS YOU CAN MAKE YOUR DAY EVEN BETTER TOMORROW. YOU CAN WRITE A TO DO LIST. THE DAY WILL GO MUCH SMOOTHER!**
- **ALWAYS SHARE** YOUR THOUGHTS AND CONCERNS WITH YOUR LOVING FAMILY FOR PROPER GUIDANCE AND GREAT IDEAS. WRITE THEM DOWN BELOW IF NEEDED.

Date ___/___/20__

Sad moments…

_____

_____

Happy moments...

_____

_____

_____

Family Bonding Time…

- **WRITE OR DRAW SOMETHING FUNNY IN THE SPACE BELOW** THAT WILL PUT A HUGE SMILE ON YOUR FACE. ALWAYS TRY TO GO TO BED SMILING AND FEELING HAPPY!
- **THINK OF WAYS YOU CAN MAKE YOUR DAY EVEN BETTER TOMORROW.** YOU CAN WRITE A TO DO LIST. THE DAY WILL GO MUCH SMOOTHER!
- **ALWAYS SHARE** YOUR THOUGHTS AND CONCERNS WITH YOUR LOVING FAMILY FOR PROPER GUIDANCE AND GREAT IDEAS. WRITE THEM DOWN BELOW IF NEEDED.

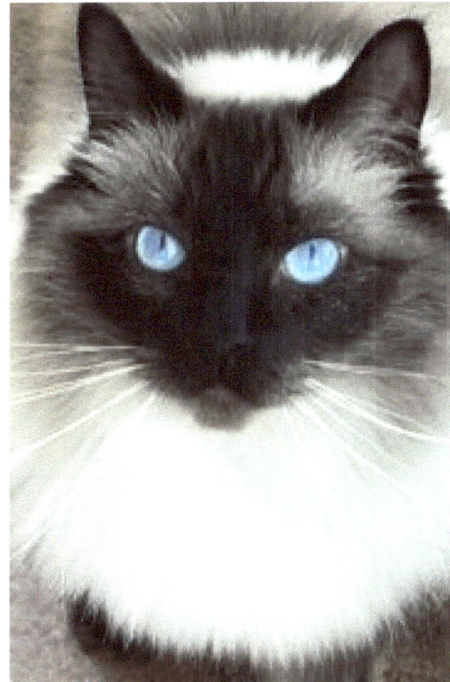

Date ___/___/20__

Sad moments…

_____

_____

Happy moments...

_____

_____

_____

Family Bonding Time…

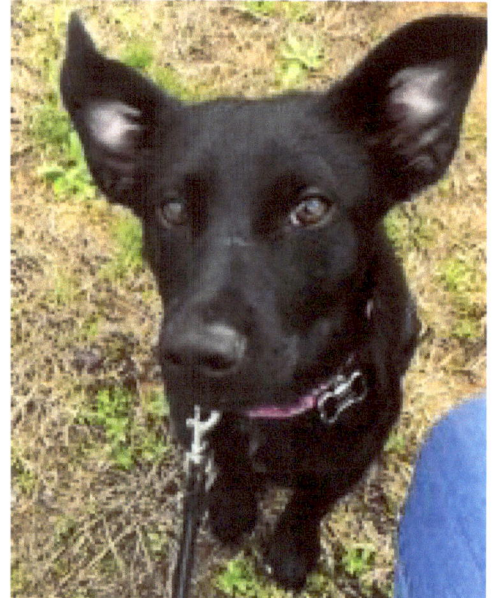

- **WRITE OR DRAW SOMETHING FUNNY IN THE SPACE BELOW** THAT WILL PUT A HUGE SMILE ON YOUR FACE. ALWAYS TRY TO GO TO BED SMILING AND FEELING HAPPY!
- **THINK OF WAYS YOU CAN MAKE YOUR DAY EVEN BETTER TOMORROW. YOU CAN WRITE A TO DO LIST. THE DAY WILL GO MUCH SMOOTHER!**
- **ALWAYS SHARE** YOUR THOUGHTS AND CONCERNS WITH YOUR LOVING FAMILY FOR PROPER GUIDANCE AND GREAT IDEAS. WRITE THEM DOWN BELOW IF NEEDED.

Date ___/___/20__

Sad moments…

_____

_____

Happy moments...

_____

_____

_____

Family Bonding Time…

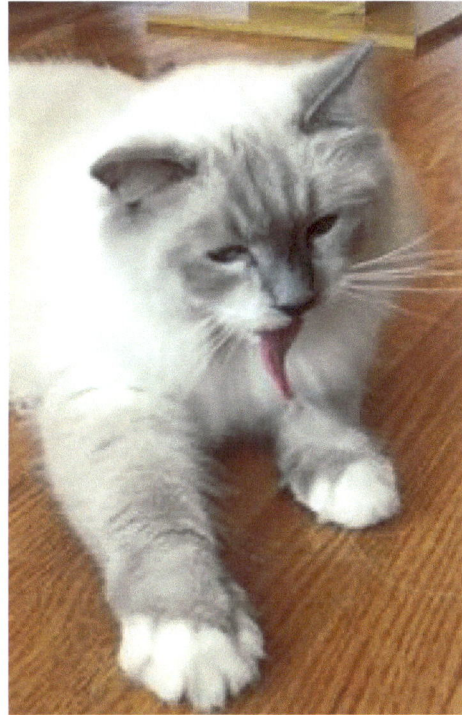

- **WRITE OR DRAW SOMETHING FUNNY IN THE SPACE BELOW** THAT WILL PUT A HUGE SMILE ON YOUR FACE. ALWAYS TRY TO GO TO BED SMILING AND FEELING HAPPY!
- **THINK OF WAYS YOU CAN MAKE YOUR DAY EVEN BETTER TOMORROW. YOU CAN WRITE A TO DO LIST. THE DAY WILL GO MUCH SMOOTHER!**
- **ALWAYS SHARE** YOUR THOUGHTS AND CONCERNS WITH YOUR LOVING FAMILY FOR PROPER GUIDANCE AND GREAT IDEAS. WRITE THEM DOWN BELOW IF NEEDED.

Date ___/___/20__

Sad moments…

_____

_____

Happy moments...

_____

_____

_____

Family Bonding Time…

- **WRITE OR DRAW SOMETHING FUNNY IN THE SPACE BELOW** THAT WILL PUT A HUGE SMILE ON YOUR FACE. ALWAYS TRY TO GO TO BED SMILING AND FEELING HAPPY!
- **THINK OF WAYS YOU CAN MAKE YOUR DAY EVEN BETTER TOMORROW. YOU CAN WRITE A TO DO LIST. THE DAY WILL GO MUCH SMOOTHER!**
- **ALWAYS SHARE** YOUR THOUGHTS AND CONCERNS WITH YOUR LOVING FAMILY FOR PROPER GUIDANCE AND GREAT IDEAS. WRITE THEM DOWN BELOW IF NEEDED.

Date ___/___/20__

Sad moments…

_____

_____

Happy moments...

_____

_____

_____

Family Bonding Time…

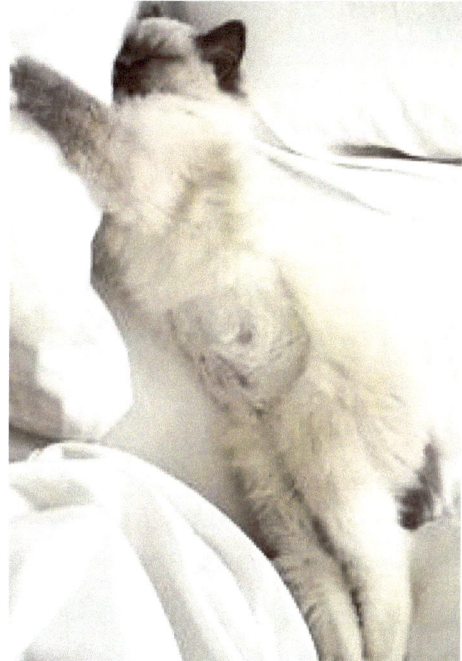

- **WRITE OR DRAW SOMETHING FUNNY IN THE SPACE BELOW** THAT WILL PUT A HUGE SMILE ON YOUR FACE. ALWAYS TRY TO GO TO BED SMILING AND FEELING HAPPY!
- **THINK OF WAYS YOU CAN MAKE YOUR DAY EVEN BETTER TOMORROW.** YOU CAN WRITE A TO DO LIST. THE DAY WILL GO MUCH SMOOTHER!
- **ALWAYS SHARE** YOUR THOUGHTS AND CONCERNS WITH YOUR LOVING FAMILY FOR PROPER GUIDANCE AND GREAT IDEAS. WRITE THEM DOWN BELOW IF NEEDED.

Date ___/___/20__

Sad moments...

_____

_____

Happy moments...

_____

_____

_____

Family Bonding Time...

- **WRITE OR DRAW SOMETHING FUNNY IN THE SPACE BELOW** THAT WILL PUT A HUGE SMILE ON YOUR FACE. ALWAYS TRY TO GO TO BED SMILING AND FEELING HAPPY!
- **THINK OF WAYS YOU CAN MAKE YOUR DAY EVEN BETTER TOMORROW. YOU CAN WRITE A TO DO LIST. THE DAY WILL GO MUCH SMOOTHER!**
- **ALWAYS SHARE** YOUR THOUGHTS AND CONCERNS WITH YOUR LOVING FAMILY FOR PROPER GUIDANCE AND GREAT IDEAS. WRITE THEM DOWN BELOW IF NEEDED.

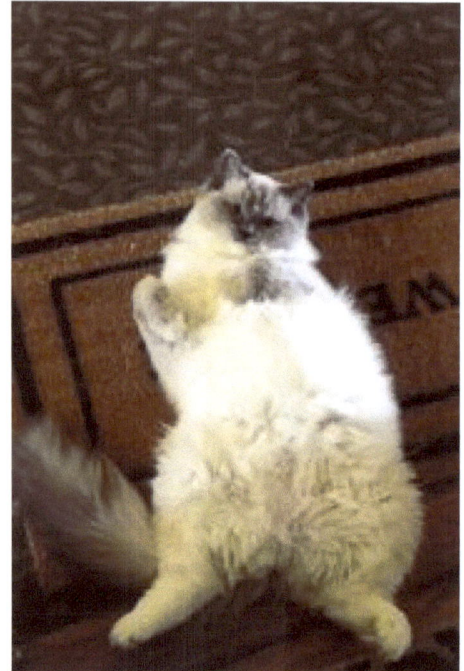

Date ___/___/20__

Sad moments…

_____

_____

Happy moments...

_____

_____

_____

Family Bonding Time…

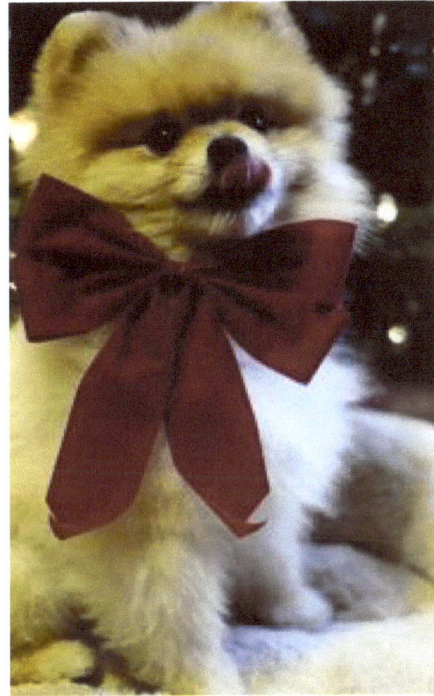

- **WRITE OR DRAW SOMETHING FUNNY IN THE SPACE BELOW** THAT WILL PUT A HUGE SMILE ON YOUR FACE. ALWAYS TRY TO GO TO BED SMILING AND FEELING HAPPY!
- **THINK OF WAYS YOU CAN MAKE YOUR DAY EVEN BETTER TOMORROW. YOU CAN WRITE A TO DO LIST. THE DAY WILL GO MUCH SMOOTHER!**
- **ALWAYS SHARE** YOUR THOUGHTS AND CONCERNS WITH YOUR LOVING FAMILY FOR PROPER GUIDANCE AND GREAT IDEAS. WRITE THEM DOWN BELOW IF NEEDED.

Date ___/___/20__

Sad moments...

_____

_____

Happy moments...

_____

_____

_____

Family Bonding Time...

- **WRITE OR DRAW SOMETHING FUNNY IN THE SPACE BELOW** THAT WILL PUT A HUGE SMILE ON YOUR FACE. ALWAYS TRY TO GO TO BED SMILING AND FEELING HAPPY!
- **THINK OF WAYS YOU CAN MAKE YOUR DAY EVEN BETTER TOMORROW. YOU CAN WRITE A TO DO LIST. THE DAY WILL GO MUCH SMOOTHER!**
- **ALWAYS SHARE** YOUR THOUGHTS AND CONCERNS WITH YOUR LOVING FAMILY FOR PROPER GUIDANCE AND GREAT IDEAS. WRITE THEM DOWN BELOW IF NEEDED.

Date ___/___/20__

Sad moments...

_____

_____

Happy moments...

_____

_____

_____

Family Bonding Time...

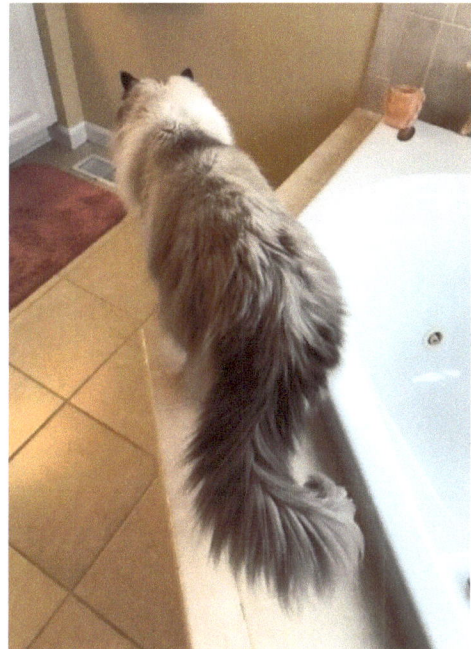

- **WRITE OR DRAW SOMETHING FUNNY IN THE SPACE BELOW** THAT WILL PUT A HUGE SMILE ON YOUR FACE. ALWAYS TRY TO GO TO BED SMILING AND FEELING HAPPY!
- **THINK OF WAYS YOU CAN MAKE YOUR DAY EVEN BETTER TOMORROW. YOU CAN WRITE A TO DO LIST. THE DAY WILL GO MUCH SMOOTHER!**
- **ALWAYS SHARE** YOUR THOUGHTS AND CONCERNS WITH YOUR LOVING FAMILY FOR PROPER GUIDANCE AND GREAT IDEAS. WRITE THEM DOWN BELOW IF NEEDED.

Date ___/___/20__

Sad moments...

_____

_____

Happy moments...

_____

_____

_____

Family Bonding Time...

- **WRITE OR DRAW SOMETHING FUNNY IN THE SPACE BELOW** THAT WILL PUT A HUGE SMILE ON YOUR FACE. ALWAYS TRY TO GO TO BED SMILING AND FEELING HAPPY!
- **THINK OF WAYS YOU CAN MAKE YOUR DAY EVEN BETTER TOMORROW. YOU CAN WRITE A TO DO LIST. THE DAY WILL GO MUCH SMOOTHER!**
- **ALWAYS SHARE** YOUR THOUGHTS AND CONCERNS WITH YOUR LOVING FAMILY FOR PROPER GUIDANCE AND GREAT IDEAS. WRITE THEM DOWN BELOW IF NEEDED.

ANSWERS

The Mother and Daughter Team would like to tell you a little bit more about our beautiful furry friends that you met during your vacation!

HERE THEY ARE:

Hippy - 14 years young Shih Tzu

- 2.5 years young Ragdoll

Gatsby - 1.5 years young Ragdoll

Emma - 5 months young rescue Lab mix

Charlie - 5 years young Morkie

Stella - 1.5 years young Ragdoll

Frankie - 2.5 years young Ragdoll

Louis - 3 years young Pomeranian

Lola - 2 years young mini Ragdoll

Kekkei - 2 years young English Bulldog

and Frankie - brothers from the same litter. Gatsby is a cousin to both of them.

OK, OK... THE ANSWERS:

~ Page 10 - Stella
~ Page 11 - Kekkei
~ Page 12 - Louis
~ Page 13 - Stella
~ Page 14 - Charlie and Hippy
~ Page 15 - Louis and Frankie
~ Page 16 - Vinny
~ Page 17 - Emma
~ Page 18 - Lola
~ Page 19 - Gatsby
~ Page 20 - Frankie
~ Page 21 - Louis
~ Page 22 - Lola
~ Page 23 - Stella
~ Page 24 - Kekkei
~ Page 25 - Louis
~ Page 26 - Charlie
~ Page 27 - Hippy
~ Page 28 - Vinny
~ Page 29 - Frankie
~ Page 30 - Emma
~ Page 31 - Gatsby
~ Page 32 - Kekkei
~ Page 33 - Lola
~ Page 34 - Kekkei
~ Page 35 - Stella
~ Page 36 - Louis
~ Page 37 - Charlie
~ Page 38 - Frankie
~ Page 39 - Emma
~ Page 40 - Gatsby
~ Page 41 - Louis
~ Page 42 - Lola
~ Page 43 - Frankie
~ Page 44 - Stella
~ Page 45 - Kekkei
~ Page 46 - Louis
~ Page 47 - Charlie
~ Page 48 - Hippy
~ Page 49 - Frankie
~ Page 50- Gatsby
~ Page 51 - Kekkei
~ Page 52 - Lola
~ Page 53 - Stella

The FURRY TEAM would like to thank YOU for a wonderful time spent with us, and we wish YOU all the luck and happiness for the upcoming school year!!!

LOVE AND PEACE

www.ingramcontent.com/pod-product-compliance
Lightning Source LLC
Chambersburg PA
CBHW060821270326
41931CB00002B/47